Rediscovering Inner Medicine

Embracing Earth's Healing Power

Welcome to "Ancient Remedies for Alignment," a guide that blends **timeless wisdom** and modern practices, inviting you to explore herbal remedies and mindful living in harmony with nature.

There is an ancient rhythm woven through every living thing — a pulse that guides oceans, seasons, and the beating of our own hearts. Somewhere along the way, the modern world taught us to move faster than that rhythm. We traded intuition for logic, nature for convenience, and stillness for striving.
But the body remembers. The spirit remembers. And when we pause long enough to listen — healing begins.
Ancient Remedies for Alignment is a return to that remembrance.

Book Vision

A beautiful, practical guide for re-balancing energy, emotions, and wellbeing — the modern wellness seeker's manual to ancient herbal, energetic, and ritual remedies.

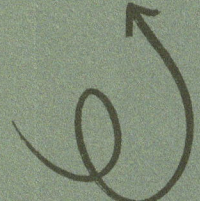

Foundations in Ancient Wisdom

Exploring Holistic Traditions for Wellness

Each entry blends ancient wisdom (Ayurveda, Chinese medicine, Indigenous practices, crystal therapy) with modern holistic science (nervous system, hormones, emotional regulation).

From the Ayurvedic rishis to Indigenous healers, from Traditional Chinese Medicine to ancient Egyptian botanists — every culture held a sacred relationship with the Earth. They understood that plants carry not only nutrients, but frequency — vibrations that speak the same language as our energy centers.

They also knew that alignment wasn't only about what we consume, but what we think, breathe, and believe.
   A simple breath could rewire the mind.
   A ritual could re-center the heart.
   A tea leaf could open the pathway to peace.

In the rush of modern life, these truths became whispers — and this book is your invitation to listen again.

Ancient Traditions

Foundations of Wellness Practices

Ayurveda

Ayurveda emphasizes balance through understanding doshas, utilizing herbal remedies to promote holistic wellness and maintain health by aligning with individual body profiles and natural cycles.

Chinese Medicine

Chinese Medicine focuses on qi flow and meridians, integrating herbal formulas to restore balance in the body, mind, and spirit, fostering overall harmony through mindful practices.

Sacred Earth Rituals

Sacred Earth Rituals foster a deep connection with nature's cycles, incorporating elemental energies into daily life, and encouraging holistic approaches to personal wellness through mindful engagement.

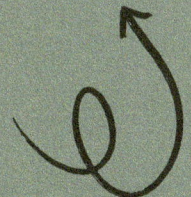

How to Use

This is not a cover-to-cover read; it's a companion. Keep it beside your tea cup, on your altar, or near your bed. When you feel off-center, open to the chapter that calls to you.

Each remedy follows a simple flow:
Symptom or Imbalance – what you're feeling or noticing.

Element & Energy Center – the energetic root of the imbalance.

Ancient Remedy – a natural approach using herbs, oils, or rituals from time-honored traditions.

Modern Alignment Practice – a grounding ritual, journaling prompt, or mindfulness tool for integration.

Mantra – a short affirmation to rewire your mind-body connection.

You can use these remedies daily, or intuitively as needed. Think of each as a conversation between your inner world and the natural world — a remembrance that healing is always available.

Your Body as a Compass

Every symptom is a message.
Anxiety is the call of an ungrounded root. Fatigue is the whisper of a burnt-out flame. Disconnection is the longing of your spirit to feel again.

Through awareness, ritual, and ancient support, we decode these messages — transforming imbalance into wisdom.

When you honor your body as your guide, you awaken the healer within.

Understanding Your Chakra System

Exploring Energy Centers for Balance

Discover the connection to wellness and harmony

Your physical body is the visible expression of an invisible energy system — an intelligent network of currents that move life force (prana, chi) through every organ, emotion, and thought.

This system flows through seven primary energy centers, known as chakras, each carrying unique frequencies and lessons.

When balanced, energy flows with ease. When blocked or overactive, dis-ease appears — emotionally, mentally, or physically.

The Seven Energy Centers

Root (Muladhara) sits at the base of the spine and represents our foundation — the energy of safety, stability, and belonging. When this chakra is balanced, you feel calm, grounded, and secure in your place in the world. When out of alignment, it often expresses as anxiety, fear, or restlessness — the body's call to reconnect with the Earth and your sense of support.

Sacral (Svadhisthana) is located in the lower abdomen and governs creativity, pleasure, and relationships.
When balanced, it flows with emotional vitality, connection, and joy. When out of alignment, it can show up as numbness, guilt, or emotional detachment — signs that your creative and emotional waters need movement and warmth.

Solar Plexus (Manipura) lies between the navel and the ribs, embodying confidence, willpower, and self-worth.
When in balance, it fuels purpose, empowerment, and inner strength. When unbalanced, it can feel like fatigue, self-doubt, or a loss of direction — reminding you to rekindle your inner fire and stand in your truth.

Heart (Anahata) rests at the center of the chest and governs love, compassion, and connection. A balanced heart chakra radiates openness, forgiveness, and empathy. When misaligned, it may manifest as grief, resentment, or emotional heaviness — an invitation to release what weighs you down and reopen to love.

5

Understanding Your Chakra System

Exploring Energy Centers for Balance

Discover the connection to wellness and harmony

The Seven Energy Centers

Throat (Vishuddha) is located at the throat and represents communication, expression, and truth. When in balance, it allows you to speak authentically and express your inner world with ease. When blocked, it can create suppression, tension, or difficulty voicing your needs — a signal to breathe deeply and give your truth sound.

Third Eye (Ajna) sits between the eyebrows and governs intuition, clarity, and inner vision. A balanced third eye brings insight, awareness, and trust in your inner knowing. When out of alignment, it can appear as confusion, mental fog, or overthinking — a reminder to quiet the mind so wisdom can be heard.

Crown (Sahasrara) rests at the top of the head and connects you to spirit, consciousness, and divine guidance.
When balanced, it brings a sense of peace, inspiration, and unity with all life. When blocked or imbalanced, it may feel like isolation, disconnection, or apathy — an invitation to return to stillness and remember your inherent connection to the divine.

These energy centers are dynamic — they respond to thoughts, foods, environments, and emotions.
Each remedy in this book helps recalibrate one or more chakras through herbs, breath, or ritual, restoring harmony to the system.

TrueJoy Teaching: The body heals when energy moves. Every breath, herb, and ritual is an invitation for movement — not perfection.

Elemental Alignment

Embracing Nature's Cycles for Wellness

Everything in existence — including you — is made of five essential elements: Earth, Water, Fire, Air, and Ether (Space).
These elements shape your physical health, mood, and energetic balance. Ancient traditions from Ayurveda to Taoism observed that imbalance in any element reflects as imbalance in life.

The Five Elements and Their Influence

Earth is the element of grounding, nourishment, and stability. It forms the structure of our bodies — our bones, muscles, and foundation — and gives us the strength to stand firm in life. When Earth energy is balanced, we feel safe, supported, and deeply rooted in our purpose. When it becomes excessive, we may feel heavy or stuck; when depleted, we become unsteady or disconnected. Simple acts like walking barefoot, eating warm nourishing foods, or sipping herbal teas such as ginger or ashwagandha restore the Earth within us.

Water is the element of flow, adaptability, and emotion. It moves through the body as blood, lymph, and creative energy — teaching us to soften and allow movement. When Water is balanced, we feel emotionally fluid, connected, and inspired.
When out of harmony, we may feel overwhelmed, clingy, or emotionally numb. **Restoring balance comes through hydration, movement, time near water, or sensual, creative expression that lets feeling move freely again.**

Fire represents transformation, digestion, and willpower. It fuels metabolism, passion, and purpose — the spark that turns ideas into action. When Fire burns evenly, we feel motivated, confident, and full of vitality.
Too much fire leads to irritation, anger, or burnout; too little causes fatigue and loss of drive.
Cooling herbs like mint and hibiscus, rest, and mindful breathing help temper excessive fire, while sunlight and movement gently rekindle it when it's dim.

Elemental Alignment

Embracing Nature's Cycles for Wellness

The Five Elements and Their Influence

Air is the element of breath, movement, and clarity. It circulates through the lungs and nervous system, carrying inspiration and mental agility. When balanced, Air brings lightness, curiosity, and flexibility. When disturbed, it can scatter our thoughts, create anxiety, or make us feel ungrounded. Slow breathing, grounding foods, and stillness anchor the Air element, turning restlessness into inspired presence.

Ether (Space) is the element of expansion and connection — the unseen field that holds all the others. It lives in silence, intuition, and spirit. When Ether is balanced, we feel spacious, intuitive, and connected to something greater than ourselves. When imbalanced, we may feel empty, isolated, or lost in thought.

Meditation, journaling, and quiet time in nature restore harmony to Ether, reminding us that spaciousness is not emptiness — it is possibility.

"The elements are not separate from you; they are you. Balance them, and you return to your natural state of wholeness."

Seasons, Cycles & Rhythms

Honoring the Natural Flow Within and Around You "The Earth moves in rhythm — and so do you. When you live in harmony with her cycles, your body, mind, and spirit remember how to rest, rise, and renew." — TrueJoy-Living

Every living thing moves through cycles — inhale and exhale, sunrise and sunset, creation and rest. The same rhythm that turns the seasons of the Earth turns within you. Your body, your emotions, your energy — all are guided by nature's quiet pulse.
When we lose touch with these rhythms, we feel rushed, scattered, or perpetually "behind." When we remember them, life begins to unfold with ease. The ancients lived by these natural patterns, and through them, they found alignment not only in body but in soul.

Below are three rhythms to return to: the daily, the lunar, and the seasonal.

The Daily Rhythm — The Breath of the Sun
Every day offers its own cycle of expansion and contraction — a mirror of your own internal tides.

Morning (Sunrise): The body awakens with Earth and Air energy. This is the time for grounding practices —
breath work, warm water with lemon, a few moments of sunlight on your skin. Set your tone, not your pace.

Midday (Sun Peak): Fire energy rises — digestion, focus, productivity. This is the time to take your heaviest meal,
to act, to create, and to move forward. Your energy burns brightest now; use it wisely.

Evening (Sunset): As light softens, Water and Ether guide you inward. Slow your breathing, dim your lights, and
release the day. Warm teas, gentle stretches, or gratitude journaling help your system prepare for rest.

Night (Moonrise): The realm of dreams, intuition, and repair. The nervous system resets; the subconscious speaks.
Protect your rest as sacred — it is your body's natural medicine.

"When you honor the small cycles, the larger ones begin to align."

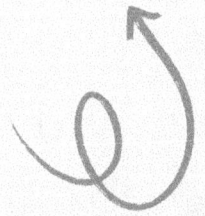

Seasons, Cycles & Rhythms

The Lunar Rhythm — The Wisdom of the Moon

The moon reflects the emotional body — its fullness and emptiness, its ebb and flow.By aligning with the
moon's rhythm, you honor your inner tides.

New Moon: A time for stillness, reflection, and planting seeds of intention. Energy is low and introspective —
rest, journal, and set quiet goals.

Waxing Moon: Growth and expansion begin. Creativity, planning, and new ideas take form. Support with
energizing herbs like ginseng or citrus.

Full Moon: Illumination and release. Emotions heighten and awareness expands. Practice gratitude,
meditation, and heart-centered rituals. Drink cooling teas like hibiscus or mint to soothe intensity.

Waning Moon: A gentle period of clearing and completion.Detoxify your space, mind, and body.
Use grounding practices and herbs like dandelion or tulsi to prepare for renewal.

"Your emotions are lunar — they do not demand control, only understanding."

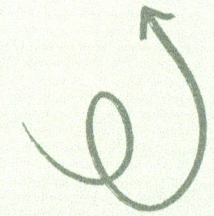

Seasonal Cycle

The Seasonal Rhythm — The Dance of the Elements

Each season carries a message — an elemental balance that teaches you how to live in harmony with change. *"The seasons are your teachers. Each one whispers what your soul needs to hear next."*

Living in Rhythm

To live in rhythm is to stop resisting your own nature.

It is to understand that life's flow — expansion, contraction, bloom, decay — is not chaos, but choreography. When you sync your lifestyle, remedies, and reflections with these rhythms, you become part of nature's harmony rather than its resistance.

"Alignment isn't found by forcing balance — it's remembered by returning to rhythm."

Seasonal Cycle

Spring Renewal

As nature awakens, focus on rejuvenation and growth through herbal remedies that support detoxification and vitality, aligning your energy with the fresh beginnings of Spring.

Spring is the Earth awakening — Air and Earth energy merging to bring growth. It calls for lightness, cleansing, and new beginnings. Focus on renewal, movement, and herbal tonics that clear stagnation.

Think: dandelion, nettle, lemon, and deep breaths.

Summer Expansion

Embrace the warmth and energy of Summer by integrating rituals that enhance creativity and joy, utilizing herbs that invigorate the spirit and promote social connections.

Summer burns bright with Fire and Water — expansion, passion, and connection. It invites you to live, express, and celebrate. Balance the heat with cooling rituals, hydration, and joy.

Think: hibiscus, cucumber, mint, laughter.

Autumn Release

As the leaves turn, practice release and gratitude in Autumn, using grounding rituals and herbs to reflect on the year, preparing for the introspective transition into Winter.

Autumn carries Air and Ether — release and reflection. Nature sheds what it no longer needs; so can you. It's time for simplifying routines, journaling, and gratitude.

Think: turmeric, ginger, warm soups, soft candles.

Winter Restoration

As the world grows quiet, embrace rest and reflection in Winter, nourishing your body and spirit with warm, grounding rituals and restorative herbs that invite stillness, replenishment, and inner peace before the renewal of Spring.

Winter is the deep pause — Earth and Water coming together for stillness and restoration. Rest replaces productivity; introspection replaces action. Nourish yourself with warmth, quiet, and comfort.

Think: ashwagandha, golden milk, long sleeps, silent mornings.

Natural Remedies & Rituals

Emotional & Energetic Imbalances

ANXIETY & OVERTHINKING

Element Imbalance: Air + Ether
Energy Center: Root & Heart

Ancient Remedy: Tulsi + Ashwagandha Calming Elixir
Steep 1 tsp tulsi (holy basil) and ½ tsp ashwagandha in hot water for 10 minutes.
Add a touch of honey and a pinch of nutmeg.
Drink slowly while focusing on your breath.

Tulsi opens the heart and calms restless energy; Ashwagandha roots the body and steadies the nervous system.

Modern Alignment Ritual:
Sit cross-legged, place one hand on your heart and one on your belly.
Inhale deeply through the nose for 4 counts, exhale through the mouth for 6.
Visualize roots descending from your tailbone into the earth.

Mantra: *"I am safe. I am steady. I am held."*

Natural Remedies & Rituals

Emotional & Energetic Imbalances

BURNOUT & EXHAUSTION
Element Imbalance: Fire + Air
Energy Center: Solar Plexus

Ancient Remedy: Reishi & Honey Restorative Tonic
Combine 1 tsp reishi mushroom powder with warm oat milk and a drizzle of raw honey.
Sip in silence after sunset.

Reishi nourishes the adrenals, restores the Shen (spirit energy), and replenishes life force depleted by overexertion.

Modern Alignment Ritual: Turn off all screens. Light a candle and journal one sentence:
"What can I release to restore my energy?"
Then list one nourishing thing you'll do tomorrow.

Mantra: "I release the need to push. I rest into my natural rhythm."

Natural Remedies & Rituals
Emotional & Energetic Imbalances

SADNESS & GRIEF

Element Imbalance: Water
Energy Center: Heart + Throat

Ancient Remedy: Rose & Blue Lotus Heart Tea
Brew 1 tsp dried rose petals and ½ tsp blue lotus in hot water.
Add a drop of rose water if available.
Drink while sitting near sunlight or candlelight.

Rose softens grief; Blue Lotus opens the spirit to higher comfort and divine connection.

Modern Alignment Ritual:
Hold a favorite crystal (rose quartz or moonstone).
As you breathe, imagine light expanding through your chest — in and out with compassion.
If tears come, let them flow; they are the body's prayer of release.

Mantra: *"My heart remembers love. My tears water new beginnings."*

Natural Remedies & Rituals

Emotional & Energetic Imbalances

ANGER & IRRITATION

Element Imbalance: Fire
Energy Center: Solar Plexus + Liver Meridian

Ancient Remedy: Peppermint & Dandelion Cooling Infusion
Steep fresh peppermint leaves and dried dandelion root for 15 minutes.
Add a squeeze of lemon.

These herbs cool fiery excess and support liver detoxification — both physical and emotional.

Modern Alignment Ritual:
Stand tall and shake your hands, arms, and legs vigorously.
With each exhale, release frustration from your body.
Then place both hands over your solar plexus and visualize a soft golden light calming your core.

Mantra: *"I release fire into light. My strength serves peace."*

Natural Remedies & Rituals

Emotional & Energetic Imbalances

EMOTIONAL NUMBNESS / DISCONNECTION

Element Imbalance: Earth + Water
Energy Center: Sacral + Heart

Ancient Remedy: Cacao & Cinnamon Awakening Drink
Whisk 1 tbsp raw cacao with ½ tsp cinnamon and a dash of cayenne into warm almond milk.

Sip with slow awareness of the warmth spreading through your chest.
 Cacao was used by the Mayans to open the emotional body and rekindle creative life force.

Modern Alignment Ritual:
Put on soft music and move intuitively — no choreography, just flow.
Let your body express what your mind cannot say.
Afterward, write one feeling word that surfaces.

Mantra: *"I awaken to feel. Feeling is my way back to joy."*

Natural Remedies & Rituals

Emotional & Energetic Imbalances

OVERWHELM & MENTAL CLUTTER
Element Imbalance: Air + Fire
Energy Center: Crown · Solar Plexus

Ancient Remedy: Tulsi, Lemon Balm & Gotu Kola Clarity Tea
Ingredients:
1 tsp holy basil (tulsi)
1 tsp lemon balm
½ tsp gotu kola
1 ½ cups hot water
Preparation:
Steep all herbs for 10 minutes, strain, and sip slowly while breathing mindfully.
Tulsi clears mental fog and anxiety, anchoring scattered energy.
Lemon Balm relaxes the nervous system, calming emotional turbulence.
Gotu Kola sharpens focus and restores clarity to an overstimulated mind.

Modern Alignment Ritual: Mind-Emptying Breath
Close your eyes and inhale through your nose for 4 counts. Exhale softly through the mouth for 6 counts, visualizing thoughts leaving like clouds dissolving in sky.
Repeat for 3–5 minutes, then whisper: "I release the noise and remember my peace."

Natural Remedies & Rituals

Emotional & Energetic Imbalances

EMOTIONAL EXHAUSTION

Element Imbalance: Water + Earth
Energy Center: Heart · Root

Ancient Remedy: Reishi, Rose & Oatstraw Restorative Brew
Ingredients:
1 tsp reishi mushroom powder
1 tsp dried rose petals
1 tsp oatstraw
1 ½ cups hot water
Optional: 1 tsp honey or almond milk
Preparation: Steep reishi and oatstraw for 10 minutes, then add rose petals for the final 3 minutes.
Strain, sip warm, and rest while breathing gently.

Reishi strengthens the heart and spirit, restoring emotional endurance. Rose softens grief and restores compassion toward self. Oatstraw nourishes the nervous system and rebuilds depleted emotional energy.

Modern Alignment Ritual: Heart Refill Practice
Place your palms over your heart and breathe slowly. With each inhale, imagine drawing in soft pink light. With each exhale, release heaviness and fatigue. Repeat for several minutes, whispering: *"I fill myself with gentleness and grace."*

Natural Remedies & Rituals

Emotional & Energetic Imbalances

INNER RESTLESSNESS & ANXIETY OF PURPOSE

Element Imbalance: Fire + Air + Ether
Energy Center: Solar Plexus · Heart · Crown

Ancient Remedy: Passionflower, Lavender & Ashwagandha Serenity Tea
Ingredients:
1 tsp passionflower
½ tsp lavender buds
½ tsp ashwagandha powder
1 cup hot water
Optional: a few drops rose water
Preparation: Steep passionflower and lavender for 10 minutes, then whisk in ashwagandha just before sipping.

Passionflower quiets looping thoughts and calms the mind.
 Lavender relaxes the heart and nervous system.
 Ashwagandha grounds and restores courage during transition.

Modern Alignment Ritual: Purpose Stillness Practice
Sit in silence and place one hand on your belly, one on your heart. Ask softly: "What truly moves me right now?"
Listen — not for an answer, but for peace. *"I am guided by stillness, not urgency."*

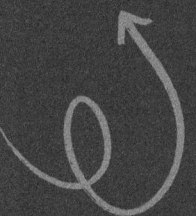

Natural Remedies & Rituals

Physical & Body Imbalances

HOT FLASHES
Element Imbalance: Fire + Water
Energy Center: Sacral & Heart

Ancient Remedy: Sage & Shatavari Cooling Infusion
Ingredients:
1 tsp dried sage leaves
½ tsp shatavari root powder (or 1 tsp dried root)
1 cup hot water
Optional: a squeeze of lemon or a few petals of dried rose
Preparation:
Combine sage and shatavari in hot water.
Steep for 10–15 minutes.
Strain and allow to cool slightly before sipping.

Sage has been used since ancient Greek times to regulate internal heat and reduce excessive perspiration.
Shatavari, known in Ayurveda as "the woman with a hundred husbands," supports hormonal balance, reproductive vitality,
and emotional cooling — bringing moisture to where the body feels dry or overheated.
Sip this infusion twice daily during transition phases — morning and early evening — to help regulate body temperature and emotional rhythm.

Modern Alignment Ritual: Cooling Breath & Emotional Soothing
When a wave of heat arises, pause and bring your awareness inward.
Place your left hand over your heart and your right hand over your lower abdomen.
Inhale slowly through the nose for 4 counts.
Exhale gently through parted lips, letting the air flow softly as if blowing over cool water.
Imagine releasing excess heat with each exhale.
Visualize silver light spreading through your heart and belly, cooling fire into calm.
Afterward, rest for a moment with eyes closed, repeating your mantra softly:
"I cool the fire within with grace and ease. My body flows in harmony."

Additional Practices & Daily Support
- Drink hibiscus and mint tea during the day to regulate internal heat.
- Add a few drops of rose or geranium essential oil to your bath for cooling aromatherapy.
- Eat hydrating foods (cucumber, pomegranate, watermelon) and reduce spicy, caffeinated, or fried foods that aggravate internal fire.
- Practice evening stillness — turn off electronics early and allow your body to cool naturally before rest.

Natural Remedies & Rituals

Physical & Body Imbalances

NIGHT SWEATS
Element Imbalance: Fire + Water
Energy Center: Heart & Root

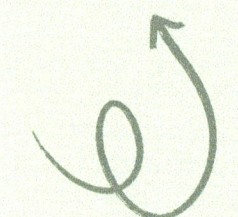

Ancient Remedy: Hibiscus, Lemon Balm & Sage Cooling Tea
Ingredients:
1 tsp dried hibiscus petals
1 tsp lemon balm
½ tsp sage leaves
1 cup hot water
Optional: drizzle of raw honey (once cooled)
Preparation:
Combine herbs in hot water and steep for 10–12 minutes.
Strain, allow to cool slightly, and sip slowly before bedtime.

Hibiscus cools and hydrates the body, supporting the heart and circulation.
Lemon Balm calms the nervous system, easing emotional tension and restlessness.
Sage helps regulate the body's temperature and reduces excessive perspiration — restoring equilibrium between fire and water within. Drink nightly for one to two weeks, particularly during hormonal transitions, to gently balance the body's cooling mechanisms.

Modern Alignment Ritual: Moonlight Breath & Cooling Stillness
As you prepare for bed, dim your lights and create an environment that mirrors moonlight — calm, quiet, and cool.
Sit comfortably and rest your hands on your knees.
Inhale slowly through the nose, imagining drawing in soft silver-blue light from above.
Exhale gently through the mouth, releasing any warmth or tension.
Repeat for several minutes, visualizing the moonlight flowing through your heart, cooling every cell of your body.
Finish by placing one hand over your heart and whispering your mantra: *"I am calm and cool. I rest in balance and peace."*

Additional Practices & Daily Support
- Keep your sleeping space cool, uncluttered, and lightly scented with lavender or rose essential oil.
- Avoid alcohol, caffeine, and spicy foods in the evening — all increase internal heat.
- Incorporate yin-based movement before bed: gentle yoga, deep stretches, or slow walks under the evening sky.
- Hydrate with room-temperature water (not ice cold) to support natural temperature regulation.

22

Natural Remedies & Rituals

Physical & Body Imbalances

HORMONAL BALANCE & MENOPAUSE SUPPORT

Element Imbalance: Water + Fire + Earth
Energy Center: Sacral · Heart · Crown

Ancient Remedy: Shatavari, Red Clover & Rose Balancing Tonic
Ingredients:
1 tsp shatavari root (powder or dried root)
1 tsp red clover blossoms
½ tsp rose petals
1 cup hot water
Optional: drizzle of raw honey or a few drops of rose water
Preparation: Combine all herbs in hot water and steep 10–15 minutes.
Strain and sip warm in the morning or midafternoon.

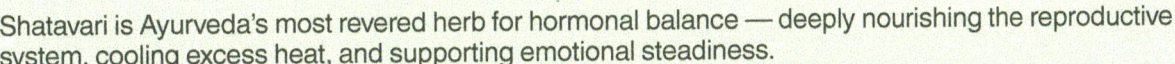

Shatavari is Ayurveda's most revered herb for hormonal balance — deeply nourishing the reproductive system, cooling excess heat, and supporting emotional steadiness.
Red Clover contains gentle plant estrogens that help regulate mood swings and temperature fluctuations.
Rose opens the heart and brings softness to the emotional body, soothing irritability and anxiety.
Sip daily for two to three weeks, especially during times of hormonal change or emotional transition.

Modern Alignment Ritual: Heart–Womb Connection Practice
Find a quiet place to sit or lie comfortably.
Place one hand over your heart and the other over your lower abdomen (womb space).
Breathe deeply, connecting the two centers with your breath.
On each inhale, imagine a soft pink light rising from your belly to your heart.
On each exhale, feel that light wash through your body, balancing warmth and calm.

Whisper gently: *"I honor my body's rhythm and trust its transformation. My wisdom deepens as my energy renews."*
Allow yourself a few moments of stillness afterward, resting in the quiet power of your evolving body.

Additional Practices & Daily Support
- Nutrition: Incorporate flaxseed, sesame, and leafy greens to support natural estrogen balance.
- Herbal Allies: Shatavari, Red Clover, Dong Quai, Vitex (Chasteberry), Maca.
- Movement: Practice gentle yoga or walking to regulate circulation and mood.
- Rest: Prioritize 7–8 hours of restorative sleep — the body resets hormonal rhythm during deep rest.
- Emotional Care: Keep a "menopause gratitude journal" — note one way your body shows wisdom and resilience each day.

Natural Remedies & Rituals

Physical & Body Imbalances

THYROID IMBALANCE
Element Imbalance: Fire + Earth + Ether
Energy Center: Throat · Solar Plexus

Ancient Remedy: Ashwagandha, Gotu Kola & Nettle Nourishing Tonic
Ingredients:
½ tsp ashwagandha powder
½ tsp gotu kola
1 tsp dried nettle leaf
1 cup warm almond or oat milk
Optional: pinch of cinnamon and raw honey for taste
Preparation:
Simmer nettle in 1 cup water for 10 minutes, then strain.
Stir in ashwagandha and gotu kola, adding warm milk.
Sweeten gently if desired and sip slowly in the morning or afternoon.

Ashwagandha supports thyroid function and balances cortisol, gently regulating metabolism and energy.
Gotu Kola enhances circulation, focus, and communication between the mind and body.
Nettle replenishes minerals, stabilizing both nervous and endocrine systems.
This tonic restores nourishment where depletion or overdrive has disturbed balance — grounding fiery energy while reawakening inner vitality.

Modern Alignment Ritual: Voice & Energy Balance Practice
The thyroid sits in the throat — the energetic bridge between thought and expression.
Imbalance often appears when words are withheld, truth is softened, or energy is overextended.
Ritual:
Sit comfortably and take a deep breath.
As you inhale, imagine blue light filling your throat.
As you exhale, hum softly — a gentle vibration to awaken the thyroid and clear stagnation.
Repeat for several rounds, letting the vibration grow stronger with each breath.

End by whispering your mantra: *"I speak with clarity. My energy flows in balanced harmony."*

Additional Practices & Daily Support
- Dietary Support: Include selenium- and zinc-rich foods (pumpkin seeds, brazil nuts, seaweed, lentils).
- Avoid excessive caffeine, processed soy, and refined sugars that overstimulate or suppress thyroid function.
- Hydrate throughout the day — the thyroid thrives in a moist, nourished environment.
- Practice gentle neck stretches and lion's breath (simhasana) to encourage energy flow through the throat.
- Use essential oils like myrrh or frankincense for topical massage along the throat and collarbones (diluted with carrier oil).

Natural Remedies & Rituals

Physical & Body Imbalances

ADRENAL FATIGUE & ENERGY RESTORATION
Element Imbalance: Earth + Fire + Water
Energy Center: Root · Solar Plexus · Heart

Ancient Remedy: Reishi, Licorice & Holy Basil (Tulsi) Restorative Elixir
Ingredients:
1 tsp reishi mushroom powder
½ tsp licorice root
1 tsp holy basil (tulsi)
1 ½ cups hot water
Optional: 1 tsp raw honey or a splash of oat milk
Preparation:
Simmer licorice and reishi in hot water for 15 minutes.
Add tulsi, cover, and steep for 5 additional minutes.
Strain, sweeten gently if desired, and sip slowly midmorning or late afternoon.

Reishi restores the body's "Shen," the spirit of calm vitality, used in Traditional Chinese Medicine to strengthen adrenal and immune function.
 Licorice root nourishes and tones the adrenals, helping regulate cortisol and blood sugar.
 Tulsi (Holy Basil) balances stress hormones, clears mental fog, and reconnects the heart with peace.
This trio harmonizes energy — neither overstimulating nor sedating — restoring your natural rhythm of vitality and rest.

Modern Alignment Ritual: Rhythmic Breath for Energy Renewal
Adrenal imbalance often comes from running beyond your natural capacity — too much doing, not enough being.
This breath helps re-synchronize the nervous system and invite balance back into the body.
Sit comfortably, feet grounded.
Inhale deeply through your nose for 4 counts.
Hold the breath for 4 counts.
Exhale gently through the mouth for 6 counts.
Pause, then repeat for 3–5 rounds.
Afterward, rest your palms over your lower ribs and whisper your mantra: *"I breathe in balance. I exhale stress. My energy restores in rhythm with life."*

Additional Practices & Daily Support
- Sleep & Rhythm: Prioritize consistent sleep and waking times.
- Avoid screens one hour before bed.
- Nutrition: Eat grounding, mineral-rich foods — root vegetables, oats, pumpkin seeds, dark leafy greens.
- Add sea salt or pink salt for adrenal support.
- Movement: Choose gentle, restorative exercises like yin yoga, tai chi, or slow walking outdoors.
- Emotional Care: Practice daily stillness — even 10 minutes of silence restores adrenal energy faster than caffeine ever could.
- Herbal Allies: Reishi, Ashwagandha, Licorice, Rhodiola, Tulsi.

25

Natural Remedies & Rituals

Physical & Body Imbalances

STOMACH ACID & HEARTBURN
Element Imbalance: Fire + Earth
Energy Center: Solar Plexus

Ancient Remedy: Aloe, Chamomile & Fennel Cooling Digestive Tonic
Ingredients:
½ cup pure aloe vera juice (unsweetened)
1 tsp dried chamomile flowers
½ tsp fennel seeds (lightly crushed)
½ tsp licorice root (optional for added soothing)
1 cup hot water
Preparation:
Steep chamomile, fennel, and licorice in hot water for 10–12 minutes.
Strain and allow to cool until warm.
Add aloe vera juice before drinking.

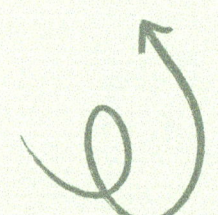

Aloe vera cools and coats the digestive tract, reducing inflammation and excess acidity.
Chamomile calms both the stomach and the nervous system, easing tension-related flare-ups.
Fennel aids digestion, relieving bloating and acid reflux.
Licorice root (optional) protects and restores the stomach lining.
Sip this tonic slowly after meals or at the first sign of discomfort to balance inner fire without extinguishing digestion.

Modern Alignment Ritual: Cooling Breath & Digestive Calm
When you feel heat rise through your chest or throat, pause for a moment.
Sit upright, place your hand over your upper abdomen, and breathe gently.
Inhale through your nose for 4 counts, imagining drawing in cool, calm air.
Exhale softly through pursed lips, visualizing releasing excess fire and pressure.
Repeat this breath for 5 rounds, focusing on slow, steady movement in the belly.
Finish by placing your palms over your Solar Plexus and repeating: *"I cool my inner fire into balance. My digestion*
flows in calm harmony."

Additional Practices & Daily Support
• Eat mindfully and slowly — avoid rushing, multitasking, or emotional eating.
• Favor smaller, balanced meals throughout the day rather than heavy dinners.
• Avoid triggers like coffee, fried or spicy foods, citrus on an empty stomach, and overeating late at night.
• Chew slippery elm lozenges or sip coconut water for natural cooling.
• Sit upright for at least 20–30 minutes after meals.
• Manage stress through gentle breath work, as emotional heat often manifests through digestion.

Natural Remedies & Rituals

Physical & Body Imbalances

DIGESTIVE HARMONY & GUT HEALING
Element Imbalance: Earth + Fire + Water
Energy Center: Solar Plexus · Root

Ancient Remedy: Ginger, Fennel & Cumin Digestive Tea
Ingredients:
½ tsp fresh grated ginger (or ¼ tsp dried)
½ tsp fennel seeds
½ tsp cumin seeds
1 ½ cups water
Optional: squeeze of lemon or drizzle of raw honey
Preparation:
Bring water to a gentle boil.
Add all herbs and simmer 5–7 minutes.
Strain, let cool slightly, and sip warm after meals.

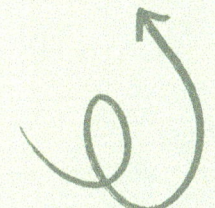

Ginger awakens digestive fire gently, enhancing circulation and metabolism.
Fennel soothes bloating and cramping while calming the gut-brain connection.
Cumin stimulates enzymes and aids the body's ability to process and absorb nutrients.
This ancient trio — used in Ayurveda as an everyday digestive support — harmonizes the gut's rhythm, restoring balance between fire (digestion) and earth (stability).

Modern Alignment Ritual: Hands-to-Belly Breath for Digestive Calm
Sit comfortably with both hands on your abdomen.
Inhale deeply, letting the belly rise into your palms.
Exhale slowly, feeling your hands soften as the breath releases.
Visualize your digestive system glowing with warm, golden light — strong yet calm.
Repeat for several minutes, allowing any tightness or tension to melt away.

Finish with this mantra: *"I digest life with ease. I trust my gut — it is my guide and my grounding."*

Additional Practices & Daily Support
- Begin each day with a glass of warm lemon water to awaken digestion naturally.
- Eat in peaceful environments — your body digests calm more easily than chaos.
- Include fermented foods (sauerkraut, kefir, miso) to nourish beneficial gut flora.
- Avoid overeating; leave a small space in the belly after meals — this supports the body's natural flow of energy.
- Take slow, mindful walks after eating to aid circulation and assimilation.
- Consider adding slippery elm, aloe, or marshmallow root if inflammation or dryness persists.

Natural Remedies & Rituals

Physical & Body Imbalances

BLOATING & WATER RETENTION
Element Imbalance: Water + Earth + Air
Energy Center: Sacral · Solar Plexus · Root

Ancient Remedy: Dandelion, Lemon & Ginger Detox Tea
Ingredients:
1 tsp dried dandelion root or leaf
3 thin slices fresh ginger
1 slice fresh lemon (or 1 tsp lemon juice)
1 ½ cups hot water
Optional: 1 tsp raw honey (after cooling slightly)
Preparation:
Add dandelion and ginger to hot water; steep for 10–12 minutes.
Strain and add lemon.
Sip warm midmorning or early afternoon to gently flush and stimulate digestion.

Dandelion supports the liver and kidneys, helping the body release excess fluid and toxins.
Ginger activates gentle movement in the gut and lymphatic system.
Lemon cleanses and balances pH, promoting clarity and lightness.
This remedy clears stagnation while grounding energy, ideal during times of bloating, sluggishness, or fluid retention.

Modern Alignment Ritual: Lymphatic Flow & Grounding Movement
When you feel heavy, swollen, or energetically stuck, move with intention.
Stand tall and begin gentle circular movements of your arms and hips.
Imagine water flowing freely through your body — no longer pooling or stuck.
Take slow, deep breaths, visualizing each exhale as a wave releasing tension.
Afterward, drink a full glass of water with gratitude.
Whisper softly: *"I release what no longer serves me.*
My energy flows freely — light, balanced, and clear."

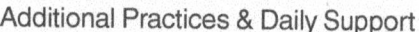

Additional Practices & Daily Support
- Begin your day with warm water and lemon to awaken natural detox pathways.
- Limit excess salt, refined sugar, and alcohol — they block water flow and increase stagnation.
- Favor light, hydrating foods like cucumber, celery, and leafy greens.
- Move the body daily — even a short walk stimulates lymphatic release.
- Incorporate dry brushing or self-massage with warm sesame oil before showering.
- Use essential oils like grapefruit, juniper, or cypress (diluted) for gentle detox aromatherapy.

Natural Remedies & Rituals

Physical & Body Imbalances

DETOX & LIVER SUPPORT
Element Imbalance: Earth + Fire + Air
Energy Center: Solar Plexus · Root

Ancient Remedy: Dandelion, Turmeric & Lemon Renewal Tonic
Ingredients:
1 tsp dried dandelion root or leaf
½ tsp turmeric powder (or ½ inch fresh root)
½ tsp ginger (fresh or dried)
Juice of ½ lemon
1 ½ cups water
Optional: pinch of black pepper (enhances turmeric absorption)
Preparation:
Bring water, dandelion, turmeric, and ginger to a gentle simmer for 10 minutes.
Strain and stir in fresh lemon juice just before drinking.
Sip warm each morning for 7–10 days during seasonal transitions or after periods of heaviness.

Dandelion cleanses and strengthens the liver and gallbladder, helping the body release toxins and stagnant energy.
Turmeric purifies the blood, reduces inflammation, and reignites digestive fire without overstimulation.
Lemon alkalizes and refreshes, clearing mental fog and fatigue often linked with sluggish liver energy.
This tonic gently awakens the body's natural detoxification systems while restoring clarity and vitality.

Modern Alignment Ritual: Fire-to-Air Breath for Cleansing & Renewal
Sit comfortably and close your eyes.
Inhale deeply through your nose, visualizing golden light entering your belly — your inner fire of transformation.
Exhale softly through your mouth, imagining that light rising through the chest and out the crown, carrying away stagnation and heaviness.
Repeat for 5–7 cycles, feeling the breath purify your entire body.
End with your mantra: *"I release the old and welcome the new. My energy is clear, my body radiant."*

Additional Practices & Daily Support
- Begin mornings with warm water and lemon to stimulate gentle detoxification.
- Incorporate bitter greens (arugula, dandelion, kale) and beets to nourish the liver.
- Limit processed foods, alcohol, and refined sugars that burden detox pathways.
- Add milk thistle or burdock root as supportive herbs for deeper cleansing.
- Move your body daily to encourage lymphatic flow and release.
- Rest deeply — detoxification happens most efficiently in stillness.

Natural Remedies & Rituals

Physical & Body Imbalances

ARTHRITIS & JOINT INFLAMMATION
Element Imbalance: Fire + Earth + Water
Energy Center: Root · Sacral · Solar Plexus

Ancient Remedy: Turmeric, Boswellia & Ginger Anti-Inflammatory Elixir
Ingredients:
½ tsp turmeric powder (or 1 inch fresh turmeric root, sliced)
½ tsp ginger (fresh or dried)
¼ tsp cinnamon
1 tsp Boswellia (frankincense resin or powder) — optional but powerful
1 ½ cups plant-based milk (almond, oat, or coconut)
Pinch of black pepper (enhances turmeric absorption)
Optional: raw honey or maple syrup for sweetness
Preparation:
Warm milk in a small saucepan (do not boil).
Add turmeric, ginger, cinnamon, and Boswellia.
Simmer gently for 5–7 minutes while stirring slowly.
Add black pepper and sweetener just before drinking.

Turmeric cools inflammation, supports joint mobility, and purifies the blood.
Boswellia (Indian frankincense) soothes stiffness and restores movement in the joints.
Ginger improves circulation and reduces swelling.
Cinnamon supports warmth and flexibility while easing pain caused by cold or damp weather.
Sip this golden elixir once or twice daily — especially in the morning and evening — to ease inflammation and restore fluidity to the body.

Modern Alignment Ritual: Gentle Flow for Release & Mobility
When pain or stiffness arises, pause and create stillness before movement.
Sit or stand comfortably and bring attention to the affected area.
Inhale deeply, visualizing warm, golden light flowing into your joints.
Exhale slowly, releasing tension and stagnation.
Gently circle your wrists, ankles, or shoulders — small, fluid motions that invite freedom without force.
Whisper softly: *"I move with ease and grace. My body is fluid and free."*

Additional Practices & Daily Support
- Hydration: Drink plenty of warm water throughout the day — dryness increases inflammation.
- Movement: Practice gentle stretching, yin yoga, or tai chi to lubricate the joints and keep energy flowing.
- Nutrition:
  - Eat omega-rich foods (flaxseed, chia, walnuts).
  - Avoid refined sugar, alcohol, and fried foods — they feed inner heat.
  - Include leafy greens, berries, and root vegetables to balance Earth and Water elements.
- Topical Support:
  - Massage affected areas with warm sesame oil infused with turmeric or eucalyptus.
  - Use Epsom salt baths for magnesium replenishment and muscle relaxation.
- Seasonal Awareness: Symptoms often worsen in cold, damp weather — stay warm, dry, and gently active.

Natural Remedies & Rituals

Physical & Body Imbalances

MUSCLE PAIN & TENSION RELIEF
Element Imbalance: Fire + Air + Earth
Energy Center: Root · Solar Plexus · Heart

Ancient Remedy: Magnesium, Lavender & Ginger Soothing Soak
Ingredients:
1 cup Epsom salts (magnesium sulfate)
½ cup baking soda
10 drops lavender essential oil
5 drops ginger essential oil (or 1 tbsp grated fresh ginger in a muslin bag)
Optional: 2 tbsp sea salt or Himalayan salt
Preparation:
Fill your tub with warm water (not hot).
Add all ingredients and stir clockwise with intention.
Soak for 20–25 minutes, breathing deeply and allowing tension to dissolve.

Magnesium relaxes muscles and releases lactic acid buildup.
Lavender calms the nervous system and eases emotional strain.
Ginger increases circulation, bringing warmth and oxygen to tight areas.
Sea salt grounds and detoxifies stagnant energy.
This ritual invites the body to unwind, muscles to soften, and the spirit to exhale.

Modern Alignment Ritual: Tension Release Breath & Self-Massage
Find a comfortable seated position.
Inhale slowly, visualizing fresh energy filling tense muscles.
Exhale through the mouth, imagining warmth melting away discomfort.
Gently massage your neck, shoulders, or calves in circular motions.
Whisper your mantra: *"I release pressure and invite peace. My body softens as my mind quiets."*

Additional Practices & Daily Support
- Hydration: Drink plenty of mineral-rich water to prevent cramping and support recovery.
- Movement: Gentle yoga, stretching, or slow walking keeps energy and lymph moving.
- Nutrition: Include magnesium-rich foods like leafy greens, almonds, and bananas.
- Topical Oils: Combine arnica, peppermint, and lavender in a carrier oil for post-activity relief.
- Rest: Allow true rest after exertion — healing happens in stillness, not strain.

Natural Remedies & Rituals

Physical & Body Imbalances

POOR SLEEP & RESTLESSNESS
Element Imbalance: Air + Ether
Energy Center: Third Eye

Ancient Remedy: Chamomile, Lavender & Nutmeg Night Elixir
Warm 1 cup oat or almond milk.
Add 1 tsp chamomile, ½ tsp lavender, and a pinch of nutmeg.
Stir clockwise three times and drink slowly before bed.

These herbs relax the nervous system and quiet mental chatter, preparing the body for deep rest.

Modern Alignment Ritual:
Dim lights 30 minutes before bed. Turn off screens and light a candle.
As you inhale, say "I welcome rest."
As you exhale, say "I release the day."
Mantra: *"Peace settles into me like moonlight on still water."*

Natural Remedies & Rituals

Physical & Body Imbalances

HORMONAL IMBALANCE / FATIGUE

Element Imbalance: Water + Earth
Energy Center: Sacral

Ancient Remedy: Shatavari & Maca Balancing Smoothie
Blend 1 tsp shatavari powder, ½ tsp maca powder, banana, almond milk, and cinnamon.
Drink mid-morning.
Shatavari supports feminine hormones and reproductive vitality; maca restores adrenal and thyroid balance for all genders.

Modern Alignment Ritual:
Place a warm hand over your lower abdomen.
Visualize a soft orange glow expanding with each breath — creative, alive, balanced.
Journal: "Where am I giving my energy away, and how can I call it back?"
Mantra: *"I am in rhythm with my body. My energy flows with grace."*

Natural Remedies & Rituals

Physical & Body Imbalances

INFLAMMATION & BODY TENSION
Element Imbalance: Fire + Water
Energy Center: Root + Solar Plexus

Ancient Remedy: Turmeric-Golden Milk Anti-Inflammatory Tonic
Warm coconut milk with 1 tsp turmeric, ¼ tsp black pepper, ½ tsp cinnamon, and a dash of ginger.
Sweeten with raw honey.
An ancient Ayurvedic blend that cools inflammation, enhances circulation, and calms body heat.

Modern Alignment Ritual:
Stretch gently or take a slow walk outdoors.
As your body moves, imagine releasing any held frustration or inflammation into the earth.
Affirm aloud: *"I soften into strength."*
Mantra: *"My body is a vessel of peace and resilience."*

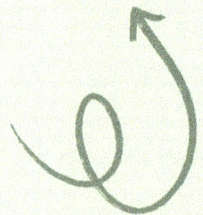

Natural Remedies & Rituals

Physical & Body Imbalances

LOW IMMUNITY & WEAKNESS

Element Imbalance: Earth + Water
Energy Center: Root

Ancient Remedy: Elderberry, Ginger & Honey Immunity Syrup
Simmer 1 cup dried elderberries, 2 slices fresh ginger, 1 cinnamon stick in 3 cups water for 30 minutes.
Strain, cool, and add ½ cup honey.
Take 1 tbsp daily during fatigue or seasonal shifts.
Elderberry strengthens the immune response while ginger clears stagnation.

Modern Alignment Ritual:
Rub a few drops of eucalyptus or tea tree oil between your palms.
Cup them over your nose and inhale deeply, visualizing protection and renewal spreading through your body.
Mantra: *"I am protected, strong, and alive with vitality."*

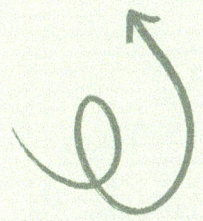

Natural Remedies & Rituals

Physical & Body Imbalances

DRY SKIN & DEHYDRATION

Element Imbalance: Water + Earth + Air
Energy Center: Sacral · Heart

Ancient Remedy: Rose, Calendula & Coconut Nourishing Infusion
Ingredients:
1 tsp dried rose petals
1 tsp calendula flowers
1 ½ cups hot water
1 tsp coconut oil or sweet almond oil

Preparation:
Steep rose and calendula in hot water for 10 minutes.
Strain and allow to cool until warm.
Stir in coconut oil until blended.
Sip a small portion as a hydrating tea, or use externally as a gentle compress on dry areas.

Rose hydrates and softens both skin and emotions.
 Calendula repairs and soothes dryness or irritation.
 Coconut oil seals moisture and calms inflamed tissue.

Modern Alignment Ritual: Self-Anointing for Nourishment
After bathing, warm a few drops of coconut or sesame oil between your palms.
Apply from feet to crown in long, mindful strokes, whispering:
"I tend to myself with love.
 I am hydrated, whole, and radiant."
Take three slow breaths, letting gratitude sink into your skin.

Additional Practices & Daily Support
• Drink warm water with lemon throughout the day to hydrate from within.
• Add omega-rich foods (avocado, flaxseed, olive oil).
• Avoid very hot showers and harsh soaps.
• Use a humidifier or bowls of water near heat sources during dry months.
• Moisturize immediately after bathing to lock in moisture.

Natural Remedies & Rituals

Physical & Body Imbalances

SORE FEET & FATIGUE

Element Imbalance: Earth + Water
Energy Center: Root · Sacral

Ancient Remedy: Epsom, Peppermint & Rosemary Revitalizing Foot Soak
Ingredients:
½ cup Epsom salts
1 tbsp sea salt
5 drops peppermint essential oil
3 drops rosemary essential oil
Optional: handful of fresh mint or basil leaves

Preparation:
Fill a basin with warm (not hot) water.
Add salts and oils, stirring clockwise with intention.
Soak feet for 15–20 minutes while breathing slowly.

Epsom salts ease muscle tension and draw out fatigue.
Peppermint refreshes, cools, and stimulates circulation.
Rosemary strengthens the connection between body and ground — awakening vitality.

Modern Alignment Ritual: Grounding Foot Awareness
After soaking, dry feet gently and apply a rich balm or sesame oil.
Massage each sole slowly, tracing the arch and heel, whispering:
"I stand in strength and move with ease."
Visualize roots of light extending from your soles into the Earth, drawing up calm stability.

Additional Practices & Daily Support
- Stretch ankles and toes daily to keep circulation flowing.
- Roll a tennis ball under each foot to release tension.
- Walk barefoot on grass or sand when possible to ground energy.
- Wear supportive shoes and avoid prolonged standing without rest.
- In the evening, elevate your feet for 10 minutes to relieve pressure.

Natural Remedies & Rituals

Physical & Body Imbalances

BRUISING & INFLAMMATION

Element Imbalance: Fire + Earth
Energy Center: Root · Solar Plexus

Ancient Remedy: Arnica & Comfrey Healing Compress
Ingredients:
1 tbsp dried arnica flowers
1 tbsp dried comfrey leaf
1 cup hot water
Optional: 3 drops lavender essential oil
Preparation:
Steep arnica and comfrey in hot water for 10 minutes.
Strain and soak a clean cloth in the infusion.
Apply the warm compress to bruised areas for 10–15 minutes, twice daily.

Arnica reduces swelling and discoloration.
 Comfrey encourages tissue regeneration — known as "knitbone" in traditional herbalism.
 Lavender soothes inflammation and pain.

Modern Alignment Ritual: Gentle Restoration
As you apply the compress, breathe slowly and imagine golden light surrounding the injury.
 Whisper: "Healing flows where attention goes."

Energetic Insight
Bruises often reflect areas of the body that have absorbed impact — physical or emotional.
As the color fades, let the memory fade too.

Affirmation: "I release hurt and restore harmony. My body repairs with ease and grace."

Natural Remedies & Rituals

Physical & Body Imbalances

HEADACHES & TENSION RELEASE

Element Imbalance: Fire + Air
Energy Center: Third Eye · Crown

Ancient Remedy: Peppermint & Lavender Cooling Compress
Ingredients:
2 cups cool water
3 drops peppermint essential oil
3 drops lavender essential oil
Optional: 1 drop frankincense (for deep calm)
Preparation:
 Mix oils into cool water and soak a soft cloth.
 Apply to forehead, temples, or back of the neck for 10–15 minutes.

Peppermint relaxes tension and brings clarity.
 Lavender soothes the nervous system and relieves pressure.
 Frankincense grounds scattered thoughts.

Modern Alignment Ritual: Head-to-Heart Breath
Close your eyes. Inhale cool air through the nose, exhale warm air through the mouth.
 Imagine light descending from your forehead to your heart —
energy moving from thought to feeling.
"I release the need to control.
 Peace flows through my mind."

Energetic Insight
Headaches often arise when the mind is overloaded and the body unheard.
Softening thought restores flow.

Affirmation: "I think clearly and rest easily. Stillness restores my strength."

Natural Remedies & Rituals

Physical & Body Imbalances

BURNS & SKIN IRRITATION

Element Imbalance: Fire + Water
Energy Center: Solar Plexus · Heart

Ancient Remedy: Aloe, Honey & Lavender Cooling Gel
Ingredients:
2 tbsp aloe vera gel
1 tsp raw honey
3 drops lavender essential oil
Preparation:
 Blend all ingredients and store in a small glass jar.
 Apply a thin layer to minor burns, sunburn, or irritation as needed.

Aloe cools and hydrates.
Honey is antibacterial and speeds healing.
Lavender calms inflammation and pain.

Modern Alignment Ritual: Cooling Breath of Release
As you apply the gel, breathe in through your nose and exhale softly through your lips — as if blowing out heat.
Whisper: "I cool, I calm, I heal."

Energetic Insight
Fire transforms, but without balance it burns.
 Healing burns is a reminder to honor your passion without force.

Affirmation: "I temper my fire with compassion. My warmth heals rather than harms."

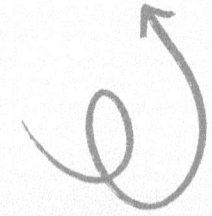

Natural Remedies & Rituals

Physical & Body Imbalances

CUTS & SCRAPES

Element Imbalance: Earth + Air
Energy Center: Root · Heart

Ancient Remedy: Calendula & Tea Tree Healing Salve
Ingredients:
1 tbsp calendula-infused oil (or olive oil + dried calendula)
1 tsp beeswax
2 drops tea tree essential oil
1 drop frankincense essential oil
Preparation:
Melt beeswax and oil together, remove from heat, stir in essential oils.
Pour into a small tin and allow to set.
Apply to clean wounds 2–3 times daily.

Calendula disinfects and encourages new skin growth.
Tea tree prevents infection.
Frankincense supports cellular renewal and reduces scarring.

Modern Alignment Ritual: Touch of Restoration
As you apply the salve, take one slow breath and thank your body for its resilience.
Whisper: "I heal quickly and completely."

Energetic Insight
Cuts remind us that boundaries were crossed — physically or energetically.
Tending them restores not just skin, but sovereignty.

Affirmation: "I am whole, protected, and healed."

Natural Remedies & Rituals

Beauty & Renewal

RADIANT BEAUTY & LONGEVITY (ANTI-AGING FROM WITHIN)

Element Imbalance: Water + Fire + Ether
Energy Center: Heart · Crown

Ancient Remedy: Amla, Goji & Rosehip Rejuvenation Tonic
Ingredients:
1 tsp amla powder (Indian gooseberry)
1 tbsp dried goji berries
1 tsp rosehip powder or crushed rosehips
1 ½ cups hot water
Optional: 1 tsp raw honey or maple syrup

Preparation:
Steep goji berries and rosehips in hot water for 10 minutes.
Stir in amla powder and sweeten gently if desired.
Sip slowly in the morning as a cellular renewal elixir.

Amla is rich in vitamin C and revered in Ayurveda for preserving youth and glow.
Goji supports collagen, immunity, and longevity.
Rosehip restores elasticity and nourishes the skin from within.

Modern Alignment Ritual: Face of Grace Meditation
While sipping, close your eyes and visualize light spreading from your heart to your skin.
Each breath becomes a pulse of renewal.
Whisper: "My radiance reflects the love I give myself."

Additional Practices & Daily Support
- Hydrate deeply — beauty begins with water.
- Sleep by 10 p.m.; skin regenerates most between 10 p.m.–2 a.m.
- Practice gentle facial massage with sesame or rose oil.
- Include colorful foods: berries, greens, beets.

Energetic Insight
Aging gracefully is remembering that time refines beauty, not diminishes it.
Your glow is a reflection of peace, purpose, and presence.
Affirmation: "I radiate timeless beauty. My light grows brighter with each season of life."

Natural Remedies & Rituals

Beauty & Renewal

NATURAL SUNSCREEN & AFTER-SUN RECOVERY

Element Imbalance: Fire + Water
Energy Center: Solar Plexus · Heart

Ancient Remedy: Aloe, Raspberry Seed & Coconut Cooling Cream
Ingredients:
2 tbsp aloe vera gel
1 tbsp coconut oil
½ tsp raspberry seed oil (natural SPF ≈ 30)
3 drops lavender essential oil
1 drop carrot-seed essential oil (for sun protection)
Preparation: Whip ingredients together until creamy. Store in a small jar.

Aloe soothes and hydrates sun-kissed skin.
 Coconut nourishes and prevents dryness.
 Raspberry seed oil provides natural UV protection.
 Lavender cools heat and calms inflammation.
Apply before light sun exposure or after time outdoors to restore balance.

Modern Alignment Ritual: Cooling Sun Recovery
After bathing, apply the cream with slow, cooling strokes from heart outward.
 Breathe deeply and repeat:
"I honor the light and rest in its warmth without burn."

Additional Practices & Daily Support
* Wear a wide-brim hat and light natural fabrics in direct sun.
* Eat cooling foods: cucumber, mint, hibiscus tea.
* For after-sun care, mist with rosewater + chamomile.
* Keep aloe gel in the fridge for quick relief.

Energetic Insight
Fire teaches vitality, yet without water it scorches.
Balance radiance with rest; receive light without losing ease.

Affirmation: "I shine with balance. My warmth is gentle, my glow protected."

Natural Remedies & Rituals

Beauty & Renewal

THICKER HAIR & LONGER LASHES

Element Imbalance: Earth + Water + Air
Energy Center: Root · Crown

Ancient Remedy: Fenugreek, Castor & Rosemary Growth Serum
Ingredients:
2 tbsp castor oil
1 tbsp coconut or almond oil
1 tsp fenugreek seeds (lightly crushed)
3 drops rosemary essential oil
Preparation: Warm base oils and add fenugreek.
Let infuse for 15 minutes, then strain. Add rosemary oil and store in a glass dropper bottle.

Fenugreek strengthens follicles and prevents breakage.
Castor oil thickens and moisturizes hair and lashes.
Rosemary stimulates new growth and circulation.
Apply a few drops to scalp or lash line (with a clean brush) 3–4 times per week.

Modern Alignment Ritual: Rooted Radiance Practice
Massage serum into scalp with intention.
 As you move your fingertips, repeat:
"I root in nourishment; growth comes with ease."
Feel warmth circulate — vitality awakening from within.

Additional Practices & Daily Support
- Brush hair gently to distribute oils.
- Eat protein-rich and omega-3 foods.
- Avoid excessive heat or chemical treatments.
- Apply serum nightly to lashes; wash gently in morning.

Energetic Insight
Hair and lashes are extensions of energy — your body's way of touching the world.
When they flourish, it reflects connection, vitality, and confidence.

Affirmation: "Growth flows through me naturally. I am strong, radiant, and deeply rooted."

Natural Remedies & Rituals

Beauty & Renewal

NATURAL BUG REPELLANT & SKIN SOOTHER

Element Imbalance: Air + Fire + Earth
Energy Center: Root · Sacral

Ancient Remedy: Citronella, Lemongrass & Basil Herbal Shield Spray
Ingredients:
½ cup witch hazel
½ cup distilled water
10 drops citronella essential oil
10 drops lemongrass essential oil
5 drops basil or eucalyptus oil
Optional: 1 tsp aloe vera gel (for skin soothing)
Preparation:
Combine all ingredients in a glass spray bottle and shake well before each use.
Spritz on exposed skin or clothing before outdoor time.

Citronella and lemongrass deter insects naturally.
Basil repels bugs while cooling the skin and soothing bites.
Aloe calms irritation and hydrates.

Modern Alignment Ritual: Protection as Presence
As you spray, take a breath and visualize a gentle golden aura surrounding you — not as defense, but harmony.
Whisper: "I move through nature with balance and respect."

Additional Practices & Daily Support
- Reapply every 2–3 hours when outdoors.
- For bites: apply lavender oil or a mix of honey + calendula.
- Keep a small bite balm (shea butter + calendula + tea tree) on hand for instant relief.

Energetic Insight
Protection doesn't mean separation — it means coexistence with awareness.
This ritual invites safety while staying open to connection with nature.

Affirmation: "I am protected and peaceful. Harmony surrounds me wherever I go."

Natural Remedies & Rituals

Beauty & Renewal

BRIGHT EYES & UNDER-EYE RENEWAL

Element Imbalance: Water + Air
Energy Center: Heart · Third Eye

Ancient Remedy: Cucumber, Rosewater & Green Tea Compress
Ingredients:
1 green tea bag (steeped and cooled)
1 tbsp rosewater
2 thin cucumber slices
Preparation:
Steep tea, cool it completely, and mix with rosewater.
Soak cotton pads in the mixture and apply to closed eyes with cucumber slices on top.
Rest for 10–15 minutes.

Green tea reduces puffiness and dark circles.
 Rosewater hydrates and soothes tired eyes.
 Cucumber cools and refreshes the delicate under-eye skin.

Modern Alignment Ritual: Eye of Clarity Practice
As you rest, inhale gently through your nose and exhale through the mouth.
 Visualize all strain dissolving — sight softening into insight.
 Whisper: "I see life with calm, rested eyes."

Additional Practices & Daily Support
- Sleep at least 7–8 hours for natural renewal.
- Massage under eyes with chilled jade roller or ring fingers using gentle pressure.
- Stay hydrated — dehydration is the silent cause of dullness.
- Reduce screen time and add daily "eye breaks" to relax focus.

Energetic Insight
Your eyes are not only for seeing — they receive emotion, light, and truth.
When you soften them, perception clears and compassion deepens.

Affirmation: "I see clearly and kindly. My vision reflects peace."

Natural Remedies & Rituals

Beauty & Renewal

HAND & NAIL REJUVENATION RITUAL

Element Imbalance: Earth + Water
Energy Center: Heart · Root

Ancient Remedy: Olive, Lemon & Lavender Nourishing Soak
Ingredients:
½ cup warm water
1 tbsp olive oil
Juice of ½ lemon
3 drops lavender essential oil
Optional: pinch of sea salt for detox
Preparation: Combine ingredients in a bowl. Soak hands for 10 minutes while breathing deeply, then massage in remaining oil.

Olive oil softens and strengthens nails.
Lemon brightens and cleanses.
Lavender soothes tension and uplifts mood.

Modern Alignment Ritual: Hands of Grace Practice
After soaking, rub palms together to create warmth. Massage oil into each finger, saying softly:
"Through these hands, I create, I give, I receive."
Visualize releasing tension and restoring flow from heart to fingertips.

Additional Practices & Daily Support
- Keep nails moisturized with cuticle oil (jojoba + vitamin E).
- Exfoliate weekly with sugar + honey scrub.
- Avoid harsh detergents; wear gloves when cleaning.
- Rest wrists and stretch fingers after long hours of typing.

Energetic Insight
Your hands are extensions of your heart — they express love, creativity, and service.
When you care for them, you honor your ability to shape your world.

Affirmation: "My hands create beauty with ease and love. I am open to receive the abundance I give."

Natural Remedies & Rituals

Beauty & Renewal

ANCIENT FACIAL RITUALS: KANSA WAND GLOW MASSAGE

Element Imbalance: Fire + Earth + Water
Energy Center: Heart · Throat

Ancient Remedy: Sesame & Rose Radiance Oil
Ingredients:
2 tbsp sesame oil
1 tsp rosehip oil
2 drops sandalwood essential oil
Optional: a few dried rose petals (for infusion)
Preparation:
Warm oil gently and, if desired, infuse with rose petals for one hour before straining.
 Use for Kansa Wand or fingertip massage.

Sesame grounds and nourishes.
Rosehip rejuvenates and brightens.
Sandalwood cools and calms fiery or irritated skin.

Modern Alignment Ritual: The Glow Practice
Apply 4–5 drops of oil to clean skin.
Using your Kansa Wand or fingers, move in gentle circular motions:
  • Forehead (clarity)
  • Cheeks (compassion)
  • Jawline (release)
  • Neck (truth)
Breathe deeply and whisper: "I lift my light from within."

Energetic Insight
Kansa metal balances skin pH and draws out excess heat — symbolic of releasing overthinking or stress.
As the skin softens, the spirit does too.

Affirmation: "I glow with harmony. Peace radiates through my presence."

Natural Remedies & Rituals

Beauty & Renewal

CLAY MASKS BY ELEMENT

Element Focus: Tailor your clay to your energy.
Energy Centers: Root → Crown

Ancient Remedy Options:
For Oily or Congested Skin (Fire Imbalance):
1 tbsp Fuller's Earth or Bentonite clay
1 tsp aloe vera gel
1 tsp rosewater

For Dry or Sensitive Skin (Air Imbalance):
1 tbsp Rose clay
1 tsp honey
1 tsp almond milk

For Dull or Tired Skin (Earth Imbalance):
1 tbsp Green clay
1 tsp lemon juice
1 tsp cucumber puree
Mix and apply for 10–15 minutes. Rinse with warm water and finish with rosewater mist.

Energetic Insight
Clay comes from the Earth — it remembers stability and draws out what no longer serves.
 Masking is a sacred act of release and renewal.

Affirmation: "As I clear my skin, I clear my energy."

Natural Remedies & Rituals

Beauty & Renewal

PUFFY EYES & FACIAL SWELLING

Element Imbalance: Water + Air
Energy Center: Heart · Third Eye

Ancient Remedy: Parsley & Green Tea Cooling Compress
Ingredients:
1 tsp chopped parsley
1 green tea bag
½ cup cold water
Preparation:
 Steep tea for 5 minutes, add parsley, and cool completely.
 Soak cotton pads and apply over eyes and cheeks for 10 minutes.

Parsley reduces water retention and inflammation.
 Green tea tones and firms the skin.

Modern Alignment Ritual: Morning Calm Practice
Keep your compress in the refrigerator and apply during morning meditation.
 Breathe slowly, repeating: "I awaken refreshed and renewed."

Energetic Insight
Swelling reflects emotion held too long — the body's way of asking for release.
As you cool and calm, you invite flow and forgiveness.

Affirmation: "I release what I no longer need. My light returns with grace."

Natural Remedies & Rituals

Beauty & Renewal

LIP & SMILE NOURISHMENT RITUAL

Element Imbalance: Air + Fire
Energy Center: Throat · Heart

Ancient Remedy: Honey, Coconut & Rose Lip Balm
Ingredients:
1 tbsp coconut oil
1 tsp beeswax or candelilla wax (vegan)
½ tsp honey
2 drops rose essential oil
Preparation:
 Melt oil and wax together.
 Stir in honey and rose oil; pour into a small tin and let set.

Rose softens emotional expression.
Honey hydrates and protects.
Coconut seals in moisture and adds radiance.

Modern Alignment Ritual: Speaking Sweetly Practice
As you apply, pause before speaking.
 Smile softly and whisper:
"May my words bring warmth and truth."

Energetic Insight
The lips are gateways of expression — the meeting place of heart and voice.
 When they're cared for, communication flows with love and ease.

Affirmation: "My words heal. My smile shines from my soul."

Natural Remedies & Rituals

Spiritual & Energetic Disconnects

FEELING LOST OR UNINSPIRED

Element Imbalance: Air + Water
Energy Center: Crown + Heart

Ancient Remedy: Frankincense & Myrrh Soul Oil
Blend 3 drops frankincense, 2 drops myrrh, and 1 tsp jojoba oil.
Rub on temples, wrists, and heart center during meditation.
Used in ancient temples to awaken divine connection and calm the wandering mind.

Modern Alignment Ritual:
Find a quiet place, close your eyes, and place your hand on your heart.
Ask yourself, "If my soul could whisper one truth, what would it say?"
Write down the first words that arise without judgment.
Mantra: *"I am guided from within. My path unfolds with purpose."*

Natural Remedies & Rituals

Spiritual & Energetic Disconnects

DISCONNECTION FROM INTUITION

Element Imbalance: Ether
Energy Center: Third Eye

Ancient Remedy: Mugwort & Sage Smoke Ritual
Burn dried mugwort or white sage in a heat-safe dish.
Let the smoke drift around your head and heart, clearing energetic noise.
 Mugwort was revered as a visionary herb, used to enhance dreams and intuitive sight.

Modern Alignment Ritual:
After cleansing, place both hands over your forehead.
Breathe deeply and visualize indigo light expanding between your brows.
Say aloud, *"I trust what I know to be true."*
Mantra: *"My intuition is clear and calm. I see with the eyes of my soul."*

Natural Remedies & Rituals

Spiritual & Energetic Disconnects

HEARTBREAK & EMOTIONAL DETACHMENT

Element Imbalance: Water + Air
Energy Center: Heart

Ancient Remedy: Hawthorn & Rose Heart Healing Tea
Steep 1 tsp hawthorn berries and 1 tsp dried rose petals for 10 minutes.
Drink slowly with both hands around your cup.
 Hawthorn strengthens the physical and emotional heart; rose invites tenderness and forgiveness.

Modern Alignment Ritual:
Hold your hand over your chest. With every inhale, imagine breathing in compassion; with every exhale,
let go of pain. Write a letter (not to send) releasing what no longer serves you.
Mantra: *"My heart is whole. Love flows freely within me."*

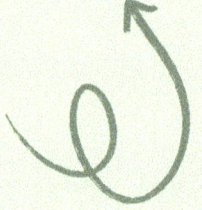

Natural Remedies & Rituals

Spiritual & Energetic Disconnects

LACK OF MOTIVATION / PURPOSE FATIGUE

Element Imbalance: Fire + Earth
Energy Center: Solar Plexus

Ancient Remedy: Ginseng & Cinnamon Vitality Brew
Steep 1 tsp ginseng root and ½ tsp cinnamon in hot water for 10 minutes.

Add a few drops of lemon for brightness.
 Ginseng restores chi (life force), reawakening drive and focus when energy feels stagnant.

Modern Alignment Ritual:
Stand tall, feet grounded.
Repeat aloud: "I am ready."
Take one inspired action — even something small — to honor your purpose today.
Mantra: *"The fire within me is steady and strong."*

Natural Remedies & Rituals

Spiritual & Energetic Disconnects

CREATIVITY BLOCK

Element Imbalance: Water
Energy Center: Sacral

Ancient Remedy: Blue Lotus & Jasmine Flow Tea
Steep 1 tsp blue lotus and ½ tsp jasmine in hot water for 5 minutes.
Sip while writing or creating.
In ancient Egypt, blue lotus was the flower of inspiration and divine pleasure.

Modern Alignment Ritual:
Sit with eyes closed and sway gently side to side, letting the body find rhythm.
Visualize orange light swirling at your hips, expanding with each breath.
Afterward, create without expectation — paint, write, or move.
Mantra: *"Creativity flows through me with ease and joy."*

Natural Remedies & Rituals

Modern World Stresses

DIGITAL OVERLOAD & SCREEN FATIGUE

Element Imbalance: Fire + Ether
Energy Center: Third Eye + Crown

Ancient Remedy: Amethyst + Sandalwood Clearing Mist
Mix 4 oz distilled water, 3 drops sandalwood oil, 2 drops lavender, and one small amethyst crystal.
Shake gently before use and mist your workspace.
Sandalwood calms the nervous system and restores presence; amethyst clears energetic clutter.

Modern Alignment Ritual:
Turn off all notifications. Step outside for five minutes.
Gaze softly at the horizon — far, not near — to reset your optic and nervous system.
Breathe deeply and stretch your fingers, releasing tension.
Mantra: *"I unplug to remember what's real."*

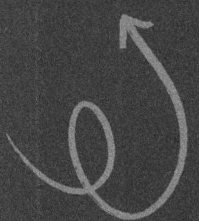

Natural Remedies & Rituals

Modern World Stresses

SOCIAL FATIGUE & ENERGETIC DRAIN

Element Imbalance: Air + Water
Energy Center: Heart + Solar Plexus

Ancient Remedy: Black Tourmaline + Salt Protection Ritual
Dissolve 1 cup sea salt in a warm bath.
Add 5 drops rosemary essential oil and place a piece of black tourmaline at the tub's edge.
Used in ancient Mediterranean cultures to cleanse and recharge the auric field after social exposure.

Modern Alignment Ritual:
After social events, take 10 minutes alone.
Sit in silence, one hand over your heart, one over your belly.
Imagine excess energy draining from your body like sand through your fingers.
Mantra: *"I release what is not mine. I return to my own calm."*

Natural Remedies & Rituals

Modern World Stresses

OVER-PRODUCTIVITY & BURNOUT CULTURE

Element Imbalance: Fire + Air
Energy Center: Solar Plexus

Ancient Remedy: Licorice & Reishi Restorative Brew
Simmer 1 tsp licorice root and 1 tsp reishi mushroom in 2 cups of water for 20 minutes.
Sip slowly mid-afternoon instead of coffee.
Both herbs were used in ancient Chinese medicine to nourish qi and calm adrenal stress.

Modern Alignment Ritual:
Schedule one "unproductive hour" each day.
No screens, no goals — simply breathe, stretch, and let your body decide what it needs.
Observe the discomfort of rest, and let it soften.
Mantra: *"I do less to become more."*

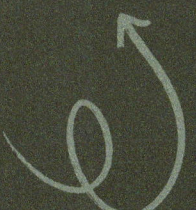

Natural Remedies & Rituals

Modern World Stresses

SELF-DOUBT & IMPOSTER SYNDROME

Element Imbalance: Earth + Fire
Energy Center: Root + Solar Plexus

Ancient Remedy: Cedar & Clove Empowerment Balm
Mix 2 drops cedarwood and 1 drop clove with 1 tsp coconut oil.
Rub on wrists and behind ears before important meetings or creative work.
 Cedar grounds; clove ignites courage and self-trust.

Modern Alignment Ritual:
Stand tall in front of a mirror.
Look yourself in the eyes and name three qualities you admire about yourself.
Repeat them aloud with conviction.
Mantra: *"I am rooted in my truth and rise with confidence."*

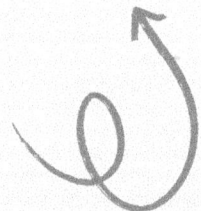

Natural Remedies & Rituals

Practical Tools for Emotional Balance

JET LAG & TIME IMBALANCE

Element Imbalance: Air + Fire
Energy Center: Crown

Ancient Remedy: Gotu Kola & Lemon Balm Re-Sync Tea
Steep 1 tsp gotu kola and 1 tsp lemon balm in hot water for 10 minutes.
Drink upon waking in your new time zone.
Gotu kola sharpens mental clarity; lemon balm resets circadian rhythm and soothes stress.

Modern Alignment Ritual:
Expose your eyes to natural light within one hour of waking.
Do gentle neck rolls and mindful breathing to align body clock with daylight.

Mantra: *"I rise with the sun. My body knows when to rest and renew."*

Integration Practices

Simple Tools for Daily Wellness

Building Your Personal Remedy Rituals

A rhythm, not a routine. Remedies work most powerfully when practiced consistently — not as a reaction to imbalance, but as a daily dialogue with the body. Your personal remedy ritual is your unique blend of herbs, breath, movement, and intention that supports your natural flow.

How to Create Your Own:

Listen to your body.
Each morning, pause and notice: Am I tired, anxious, heavy, scattered, or at peace? Awareness is the first medicine.

Identify the Element or Chakra calling for attention.
Grounding → Earth / Root
Flow → Water / Sacral
Activation → Fire / Solar Plexus
Softening → Air / Heart
Clarity → Ether / Throat / Crown

Choose your Ally.
Select one herb, oil, or ritual that balances the element.

Example: Tulsi for clarity, Rose for compassion, Dandelion for release, Ashwagandha for grounding.
Infuse it with Intention. Say aloud what you are inviting in: calm, clarity, confidence, love. Intention transforms ingredients into energy.

Anchor it in Time.
Morning → Renewal & focus
Midday → Energy & clarity
Evening → Restoration & release

Example: If you feel anxious (Air imbalance), choose Tulsi & Ashwagandha tea, breathe deeply for two minutes, and repeat the mantra: "I root into calm and move with peace."

Over time, this becomes not a remedy, but a rhythm — your signature energy of balance.

Integration Practices

Simple Tools for Daily Wellness

Creating an Alignment Corner (Home Energy Setup)

Your sanctuary of stillness. Your space reflects your state. Creating a small, sacred area — your Alignment Corner — helps anchor your daily practice. It doesn't need to be elaborate; it only needs to feel aligned.

How to Design Your Alignment Corner:
1. Location: Choose a quiet area with natural light — a corner of your bedroom, living room, or garden nook.

2. Foundation: Lay a mat, small rug, or cushion where you can sit comfortably.

3. Elements to Include:
- Earth: A plant, stone, or salt lamp for grounding.
- Water: A bowl of water, shell, or glass vessel for flow.
- Fire: A candle for transformation and light.
- Air: Incense, feather, or essential oils for breath and movement.
- Ether: A crystal, lotus symbol, or small space of open air for expansion.

4. Energy Enhancers:
- Use soft lighting — warm golden or natural tones.
- Play gentle sound (mantra, nature, or silence).
- Keep a TrueJoy Planner, Ritual Journal, or Remedy Tracker nearby.

5. Daily Use:
Visit your Alignment Corner morning and evening.
Sip tea, breathe, meditate, or write one sentence of reflection.
This simple consistency rewires energy — the nervous system begins to associate this place with peace.

"When you return to your corner, you return to yourself."

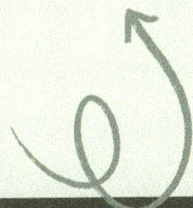

Integration Practices

Simple Tools for Daily Wellness

TrueJoy Alignment Practices

The bridge between learning and living. Your healing journey doesn't end with this book — it expands through experience. The TrueJoy ecosystem was created to help you integrate these teachings into every layer of your life.

TrueJoy Retreats:
Immersive experiences in nature where you live the remedies. Through movement, meditation, and meals aligned with the elements, you return to your natural rhythm.

The 40-Day Sādhana Practice:
A devotional rhythm for deep reset. Each Sādhana (daily spiritual discipline) blends mantra, breathwork, and meditation to regulate the nervous system and build consistency.
It helps translate the energy of each TrueJoy Pillar into a lived state. Consistency creates safety; safety creates transformation.

The Year of Transformation Program:
A 12-month guided journey that expands on this book's wisdom. Each month aligns with an element and chakra, deepening your understanding of balance in body, mind, and spirit.
Includes:
- Monthly Remedy Focus
- Seasonal Rituals
- Energy Lessons & Emotional Healing
- Nutrition & Movement aligned with the seasons

"Through rhythm, the extraordinary becomes everyday."

Each of these offerings is a living expression of the TrueJoy principle: awareness → alignment → embodiment. They are invitations to turn information into transformation.

Journaling Prompts for Self-Awareness

Reflection Pages
Integration through awareness. Healing deepens through reflection — by seeing yourself with gentle honesty.

Use these prompts to record your experiences, track remedies, and capture insights as they unfold.

These pages serve as your map — a visual dialogue between you and your evolving self.
"Every reflection is a remembrance — of how far you've come, and how naturally you were made to heal."

Weekly Reflection Prompts:

What imbalance or emotion did I notice most often this week?

Which remedy, ritual, or breath helped me return to calm?

What repeated pattern am I ready to release?

How does alignment feel in my body today?

Which element or chakra feels most alive within me right now?

What truth am I ready to speak or embody more fully?

Monthly Integration Review:

What have I learned about my energy this month?

Which remedy or ritual has become part of my rhythm?

How has my body, mood, or awareness shifted?

Where can I bring more joy, balance, or ease next month?

Closing Thought for Integration:

You are your greatest healer. The herbs, the rituals, and the rhythms are simply mirrors, helping you remember what alignment already feels like. Continue to listen — and let your life become your practice.

Journaling Prompts for Self-Awareness

Weekly Reflection Prompts:

What imbalance or emotion did I notice most often this week?

Journaling Prompts for Self-Awareness

Weekly Reflection Prompts:

Which remedy, ritual, or breath helped me return to calm?

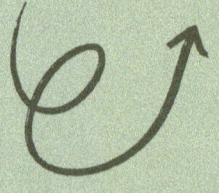

Journaling Prompts
for Self-Awareness

Weekly Reflection Prompts:

What repeated pattern am I ready to release?

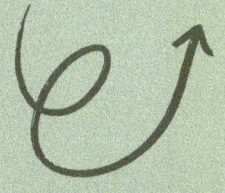

Journaling Prompts for Self-Awareness

Weekly Reflection Prompts:

How does alignment feel in my body today?

Journaling Prompts for Self-Awareness

Weekly Reflection Prompts:

Which element or chakra feels most alive within me right now?

Journaling Prompts
for Self-Awareness

Weekly Reflection Prompts:

What truth am I ready to speak or embody more fully?

Journaling Prompts
for Self-Awareness

Monthly Integration Review:

What have I learned about my energy this month?

Journaling Prompts for Self-Awareness

Monthly Integration Review:

Which remedy or ritual has become part of my rhythm?

Journaling Prompts
for Self-Awareness

Monthly Integration Review:

How has my body, mood, or awareness shifted?

Journaling Prompts
for Self-Awareness

Monthly Integration Review:

Where can I bring more joy, balance, or ease next month?

QUICK INDEX OF REMEDIES
A simple guide to finding the right ritual for your body, mind, and spirit.

HOW TO USE THIS INDEX
Follow your symptom, season, or feeling — trust what draws you in. Every remedy begins as a recipe and ends as a ritual. The most powerful medicine is awareness: the pause, the breath, the intention.

"When the body whispers, listen. When the spirit stirs, honor. Every moment of care is a return to alignment."

PHYSICAL & BODY ALIGNMENT

Arthritis & Joint Pain — Turmeric, Boswellia & Cinnamon Balm
Bruising & Inflammation — Arnica & Comfrey Healing Compress
Burns & Irritated Skin — Aloe, Honey & Lavender Cooling Gel
Cuts & Scrapes — Calendula & Tea Tree Healing Salve
Digestive Upset / Heartburn — Aloe, Fennel & Chamomile Tonic
Dry Skin & Dehydration — Rose, Calendula & Coconut Infusion
Headaches & Tension — Peppermint & Lavender Cooling Compress
Hot Flashes & Hormonal Heat — Sage & Shatavari Cooling Brew
Immune Strength — Elderberry, Ginger & Tulsi Tonic
Sore Feet & Fatigue — Epsom, Peppermint & Rosemary Soak
Stomach Acid & Indigestion — Fennel, Chamomile & Lemon Balm Tea

EMOTIONAL & ENERGETIC BALANCE

Anxiety & Fear — Rooting Breath + Tulsi Grounding Tea
Emotional Fatigue — Reishi, Rose & Oatstraw Brew
Grief & Heart Healing — Rose & Hawthorn Heart Elixir
Overwhelm & Clarity — Lemon Balm, Gotu Kola & Mint Infusion
Sleep & Restless Nights — Lavender, Chamomile & Ashwagandha Dream Tea
Stress & Nervous System — Breath Ritual + Ashwagandha Root Tonic

QUICK INDEX OF REMEDIES
A simple guide to finding the right ritual for your body, mind, and spirit.

BEAUTY & RENEWAL

Anti-Aging / Radiance — Amla, Goji & Rosehip Rejuvenation Tonic
Bright Eyes & Puffiness — Cucumber, Rosewater & Green Tea Compress
Chapped Lips — Honey, Coconut & Rose Balm
Dull Complexion — Clay Mask by Element Ritual
Dry Hands & Nails — Olive, Lemon & Lavender Soak
Hair & Scalp Health — Bhringraj, Amla & Rosemary Oil
Long Lashes / Brows — Castor & Vitamin E Growth Serum
Natural Bug Repellant — Citronella, Lemongrass & Basil Spray
Natural Sunscreen — Aloe, Raspberry Seed & Coconut Cream
Under-Eye Renewal — Rose, Green Tea & Cucumber Compress

CYCLES, SEASONS & SPIRITUAL INTEGRATION

Spring Renewal — Detox Glow Tea + Lemon Bath Ritual
Summer Expansion — Cooling Mist + Aloe Hydration Ritual
Autumn Release — Grounding Foot Soak + Gratitude Practice
Winter Restoration — Warm Sesame Oil Massage + Reishi Elixir
Aura Protection — Basil, Frankincense & Sage Spray
Cleansing Smoke Ritual — Palo Santo + Rosemary Bundle
Elemental Facial Ritual —Kansa Wand Glow Massage
Emotional Reset Bath — Rose, Honey & Milk Soak

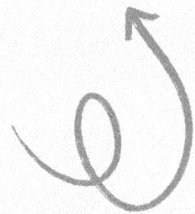

FINAL BLESSING — RETURN TO ALIGNMENT

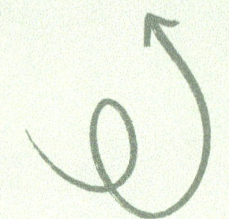

"Healing is remembering who you are beneath the noise,
and returning to that truth again and again."

May these remedies remind you that wellness is not found in any single herb, ritual, or practice —
but in your willingness to listen.

Each breath, each sip, each act of care becomes medicine when done with awareness.

The same Earth that grows your food grows your peace.

The same water that flows through rivers flows through you.

You are not separate from nature — you are nature, learning to tend to itself with love.

Let this book be a guide, not an ending.

Keep creating your own rituals of renewal, your own language of balance.
Every moment of attention is a prayer, every act of nourishment a return.

"I live in alignment with my truth. I am whole, radiant, and free."

With gratitude and grace,
— TrueJoy Living